MILITARY TECHNOLOGIES

TECHNOLOGY DURING THE
REVOLUTIONARY WAR

LAUREN KUKLA

Checkerboard
Library

An Imprint of Abdo Publishing
abdopublishing.com

ABDOPUBLISHING.COM

Published by Abdo Publishing, a division of ABDO, PO Box 398166, Minneapolis, Minnesota 55439. Copyright © 2017 by Abdo Consulting Group, Inc. International copyrights reserved in all countries. No part of this book may be reproduced in any form without written permission from the publisher. Checkerboard Library™ is a trademark and logo of Abdo Publishing.

Printed in the United States of America, North Mankato, Minnesota
102016
012017

THIS BOOK CONTAINS
RECYCLED MATERIALS

Content Developer: Nancy Tuminelly
Design and Production: Mighty Media, Inc.
Series Editor: Rebecca Felix
Cover Photo: Wikimedia Commons
Interior Photos: Getty Images, p. 6; iStockphoto, pp. 5, 8, 9, 12, 17, 18, 26; North Wind Picture Archives, pp. 23, 25; Shutterstock Images, pp. 14-15, 20; Wikimedia Commons, pp. 11, 29

Publisher's Cataloging-in-Publication Data

Names: Kukla, Lauren, author.
Title: Technology during the Revolutionary War / by Lauren Kukla.
Description: Minneapolis, MN : Abdo Publishing, 2017. | Series: Military technologies | Includes bibliographical references and index.
Identifiers: LCCN 2016945097 | ISBN 9781680784138 (lib. bdg.) | ISBN 9781680797664 (ebook)
Subjects: LCSH: United States--History--Revolutionary War, 1775-1783--Technology--Juvenile literature. | Technology--United States--History--18th century--Juvenile literature.
Classification: DDC 973.3--dc23
LC record available at http://lccn.loc.gov/201695097

CONTENTS

≡①≡
AMERICA AT WAR

In the early 1770s, many Americans were restless. At the time, America was made up of 13 British colonies. British settlers had been coming to North America for more than 150 years. But many Americans felt Britain no longer had their best interests in mind. These Americans became known as Patriots. And they were prepared to go to war.

Americans had been upset by British leadership for some time. From 1764 to 1774, Britain had passed a series of laws adding new taxes for the colonists. British leaders wanted to pay off **debt** created by British involvement in the **French and Indian War**. The colonists felt these taxes were unfair. Many protested against them.

British leaders responded by sending British soldiers to America to help enforce British laws. This upset many colonists. They continued to protest. Protests in Boston, Massachusetts, caused Britain to pass new laws punishing

the city. Colonists nicknamed these laws the Intolerable Acts. Many colonial leaders felt it was time to separate from Great Britain.

In September 1774, several colony representatives met in Philadelphia, Pennsylvania. There, they discussed a response to the British laws. This meeting was known as the First Continental Congress.

On March 5, 1770, British soldiers shot and killed five Americans during a Boston protest. This became known as the Boston Massacre. It is one of the conflicts that led to the Intolerable Acts.

British troops (*left*) face off against Patriots (*right*) at the Battle of Concord. Both sides used muskets during this early battle of the American Revolution.

Representatives wrote a **petition** at the First Continental Congress. It demanded that Britain end the Intolerable Acts. Meanwhile, the colonies began strengthening their militias and gathering weapons.

On April 19, 1775, British troops marched toward Concord, Massachusetts. Their orders were to destroy colonial supplies hidden there. On the way, the soldiers passed Lexington, Massachusetts. A group of about

70 colonial militiamen met them near this city. To this day, no one knows who fired the first shot. But it led to the first battle of the Revolutionary War, or American Revolution.

In May 1775, a second Continental Congress met. By July, its delegates had formed a Continental Army. One year later, on July 4, 1776, Congress declared independence from Great Britain. Colonial leaders formed a new nation, the United States of America.

The American Revolution would last for eight years. It was a challenging fight for colonists. Britain had an experienced army. Many American soldiers lacked military experience.

Great Britain also had a large supply of military **technology**, including weapons. At first, many Continental soldiers provided their own weapons. However, as the young United States gained foreign **allies**, it was able to obtain better weapons and technology. Military technology was much less advanced in the 1700s than it is today. Still, it was key to fighting and winning the American Revolution.

TIMELINE

APRIL 19, 1775

The first shots of the American Revolution are fired in the Battles of Lexington and Concord.

MARCH 17, 1776

George Washington and the Continental Army capture Boston from the British. This ends the Siege of Boston.

JUNE 17, 1775

Americans lose the Battle of Bunker Hill to the British. However, British battle deaths outnumber American battle deaths.

JULY 4, 1776

The Second Continental Congress declares independence from Great Britain.

OCTOBER 7, 1777

British forces surrender to Patriots in Saratoga, New York. This victory helps convince the French king to join the American cause.

DECEMBER 26, 1776

Washington leads his troops to victory at Trenton, New Jersey, after crossing the Delaware River the night before.

OCTOBER 19, 1781

British Commander Charles Cornwallis surrenders to Washington, ending the Siege of Yorktown. This is the final major battle of the American Revolution.

MUSKETS AND RIFLES

As the American Revolution began, **firearms** quickly became some of the troops' most important weapons. Muskets were the most common firearms used by both sides. To make these long, **smoothbore** guns even more **dangerous**, soldiers often attached bayonets to them.

Muskets were first used in Spain in the 1500s. They soon spread throughout Europe. When colonists came to America, they brought muskets with them. By the 1770s, most colonists owning these weapons used flintlock muskets. Flintlocks use flint and steel to **ignite** a spark that lights **gunpowder**. They are loaded with lead balls.

The musket was one of the most advanced weapons at the time of the American Revolution. However, muskets were not as **reliable** as weapons of today. They were not very **accurate** at long distances. So, soldiers often lined up in rows and fired at the same time. This way, they were more likely to hit the enemy.

Patriot soldiers fire bayoneted muskets during the 1776 Battle of Long Island.

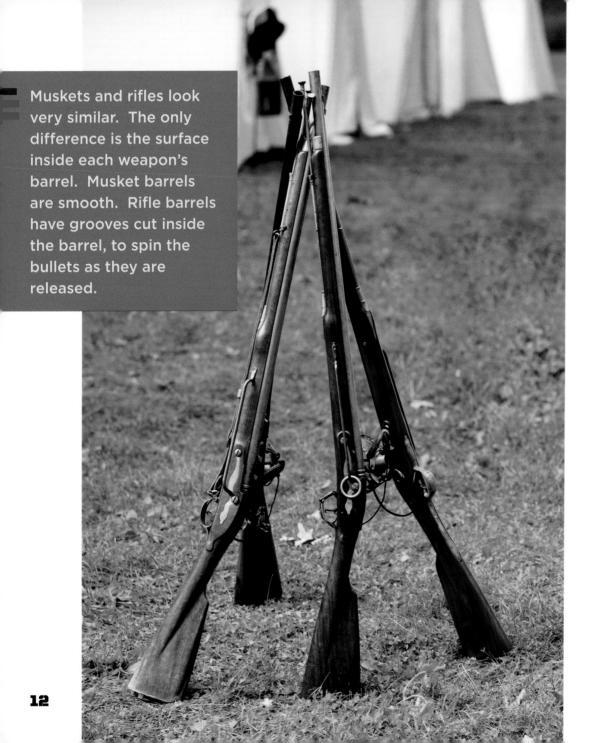

Muskets and rifles look very similar. The only difference is the surface inside each weapon's barrel. Musket barrels are smooth. Rifle barrels have grooves cut inside the barrel, to spin the bullets as they are released.

Muskets had to be reloaded after every shot. And they took a long time to load. A well-trained soldier could load a musket only three times per minute on average. The firing of many muskets also created a cloud of smoke on the battlefield, affecting soldiers' visibility.

To make more **accurate** shots, some American soldiers used flintlock rifles. Unlike **smoothbore** muskets, rifles had grooves inside their barrels. This caused the bullet to spin as it was fired, which improved accuracy. Riflemen could hit targets more than 200 yards (180 m) away.

Once American military leaders saw how accurate rifles were, they had gun manufacturers produce them for the troops. However, rifles had disadvantages too. The grooves inside their barrels made them slower to reload than muskets. It took the average soldier more than one minute to reload his rifle.

Being slow to reload was not the only disadvantage of rifles. Another drawback was that bayonets could not be attached to them. So, while rifles were better for distant shots, soldiers preferred muskets in close combat.

FLINTLOCK FIREARM

Flintlock rifles and muskets were loaded in the same way. For ease of reloading, soldiers were given premeasured paper **cartridges**. Each was filled with **gunpowder** and a lead ball. This way soldiers didn't have to measure out gunpowder in the middle of a battle.

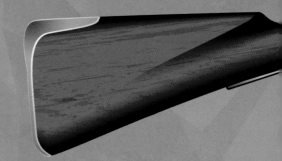

LOADING

1. First, the soldier pulled the hammer back.

2. The soldier tore off the end of the cartridge. Then he poured a little gunpowder into the pan.

3. Next, the soldier poured the rest of the gunpowder into the barrel. The soldier stuffed a bit of the paper into the barrel. This is called a wad. It held the powder in place.

4. Then, the soldier loaded the lead ball into the barrel.

5. Finally, the soldier used the ramrod to push the lead ball to bottom of barrel. It needed to sit snugly on top of the wad. Now the flintlock was ready to fire.

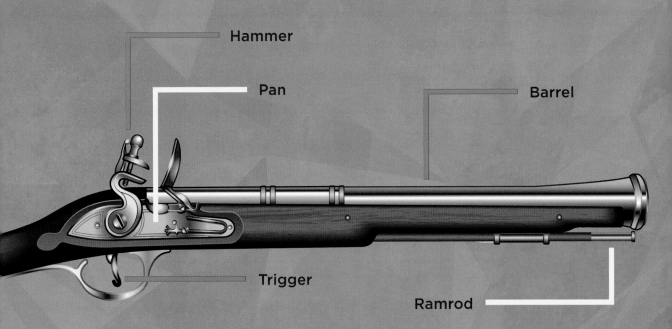

Hammer

Pan

Barrel

Trigger

Ramrod

FIRING

6. To fire a flintlock, the soldier pulled the trigger. This pulled the hammer, which held a piece of flint.

7. The flint struck a piece of steel sitting on the pan. The **friction** between the flint and the steel **ignited** a spark. The spark lit the **gunpowder** inside the pan.

8. The lit gunpowder in the pan burned through a small hole and into the barrel. This lit the gunpowder in the barrel. The lit gunpowder began heating gases inside the barrel, causing them to expand rapidly. This pushed the lead ball out of barrel at top speed.

≡③≡
ARTILLERY

Handheld weapons such as muskets and rifles played an important role in the American Revolution. But **artillery** also provided a huge advantage in battles. This included cannons, mortars, and howitzers.

Artillery was extremely heavy, making it challenging to move. But the power of these weapons was unmatched at the time. They fired much larger **projectiles**. And they fired hundreds of feet farther than a rifle's range. Artillery could also be mounted on ships for sea battles.

When the war first broke out, the Patriots had a limited supply of this artillery. They had only six small cannons at the Battle of Bunker Hill near Boston on June 17, 1775. The British had many more cannons lined up along Boston's Charles River. They won the battle that day.

American General George Washington knew his troops needed more artillery if they had any hope of winning the war. As the war continued, the Patriots gained artillery by

A cloud of smoke fills the battlefield as soldiers fire a cannon during the Battle of Bunker Hill.

capturing weapons from the British. Foreign **allies** also provided the Patriots with **artillery**. And colonists built some of their own artillery too.

On average, cannons could fire projectiles 2,000 yards (1,830 m).

CANNONS

Cannons were often used in in the field during the American Revolution. These long-range guns had lengthy barrels and wheels on them. So, they could be moved more easily than other **artillery**, which didn't have wheels.

Soldiers generally fired cannons down a straight **trajectory**. Cannonballs were the standard **projectile** for straight trajectories. These large, heavy balls bounced and rolled when they hit the ground. Soldiers also loaded cannons with canisters or grape shot.

A canister was a metal **cylinder** filled with small iron balls. When fired, the outer cylinder was destroyed, and the balls would scatter. Grape shot was a canvas bag filled with small iron balls. It worked in a similar way to a canister.

TECH FACT

Cannon is a general term that applies to many types of artillery, including mortars and howitzers. As this type of weapon became popular, *cannon* soon came to mean any gun fired from a barrel that was fixed and larger than 1 inch (2.5 cm).

MORTARS AND HOWITZERS

Two other types of **artillery** were mortars and howitzers. Mortars had short barrels and were ideal for firing over barriers. They fired shells that exploded when they hit the ground.

THE SIEGE OF BOSTON

Artillery played an important role during the Siege of Boston. It took place from 1775 to 1776. British troops took over Boston in April 1775. George Washington did not have enough artillery to force the British to leave. And the nearest cannons were more than 300 miles (483 km) away, at Fort Ticonderoga in New York.

Patriots had captured the fort from the British in May 1775. In doing so, the Americans gained 78 cannon guns, 3 howitzers, and 6 mortars. However, this heavy artillery was far away. And it was difficult to move across the mountains.

But Boston bookseller Henry Knox was up to the challenge. In December 1775, he traveled to the fort. He chose 60 cannons to bring to Boston. Knox used 42 sleds, 160 oxen, and several barges to move the artillery. He dragged the weapons across frozen, rocky, and forested landscape. The journey took 50 days.

On March 4, 1776, Washington's troops aimed their new artillery at Boston and its harbor. British fire could not reach the Patriots high up in the hills. So, on March 17, the British finally left the city.

ARTILLERY ON THE BATTLEFIELD

Howitzers had longer barrels than mortars, but shorter barrels than guns. These weapons were loaded with different types of **ammunition**. They were used to fire both shells and grape shot.

SECRETS AND SPIES

As the American Revolution raged on, information became an important weapon. If British leaders discovered Washington's battle plans, it could cost the Americans a battle. If Washington learned British secrets, the Continental Army would have an advantage. As a result, both sides spied on each other during the war.

Both British and American forces used invisible ink to pass secret messages within their troops. Troops used the ink to write messages between the lines of an unrelated letter. This way, the letter looked complete if it was captured and read by the enemy. But the invisible ink could be revealed by applying heat or chemicals to the paper.

TECH FACT

Anna Smith Strong, an American spy, was said to leave messages in laundry drying on her clothesline. She arranged the laundry to send signals to American leaders.

The British often hid secret letters inside feather quills, buttons, and small hollow balls. And Americans found ways beyond paper to pass messages. These included ciphers, which used code to change the content of a message to keep it secret.

The night before the American Revolution began, Patriots used lanterns to communicate about the British. American Paul Revere saw two lanterns in a steeple. This told him British troops were arriving by sea to invade Lexington and Concord. Revere warned the Patriots in preparation.

THE WAR AT SEA

With information and more weapons, the Americans were often victorious during land battles against the British. But success at sea was much more challenging. At the time, Great Britain had the largest navy in the world, with hundreds of ships. The Continental Navy had just seven ships when it formed in October 1775.

The Continental Navy would grow to 27 ships by the end of 1776. These included frigates, brigs, sloops, and schooners. Frigates generally had three masts. They carried either 24, 28, or 32 guns on a single deck.

Brigs had two masts and carried either 14 or 16 guns. Sloops and schooners were smaller than brigs. They usually carried between 4 and 10 guns.

PRIVATEERS

Although the Patriots had fewer ships than Britain's navy, the colonies were full of merchant ships. Many of these

ships carried guns. So, the Patriot leaders turned many merchant crews into privateers.

Privateers were people who owned private ships and were allowed by the American government to attack British ships. Privateers commissioned almost 800 ships during the war. With them, they captured about 600 British ships.

DIGGING IN

On October 7, 1777, British forces surrendered to the Continental army in Saratoga, New York. This victory helped convince the French king to support the Patriots' cause. In 1778, France joined the war as America's first official **ally**. It provided Patriots with money, supplies, soldiers, and sailors.

The French alliance was a turning point for the Patriots. In addition to troops and supplies, France taught the troops military skills. French military engineers helped Americans build earthworks and trenches. These dirt structures helped protect both soldiers and equipment during land battles.

Major General Marquis de Lafayette waves an American flag atop a trench during the Battle of Yorktown. Lafayette was one French ally who arrived to aid the Patriots during the battle.

SIEGE OF YORKTOWN

By late summer 1781, the Patriots had taken an upper hand in the war. But the British occupied Yorktown, Virginia. They built a series of trenches and ten **redoubts** to defend the city.

On September 28, French and American troops arrived in Yorktown. They got right to work digging trenches. More troops arrived. Soon, the Continental Army had nearly 20,000 troops surrounding the British.

In mid-October, the Patriots captured two of the redoubts. This was made possible because the French navy had defeated the British navy and prevented **reinforcements** from arriving. On October 17, the British surrendered on the battlefield. The Siege of Yorktown was the final battle of the American Revolution.

TRENCHES ON THE BATTLEFIELD

Trenches and earthworks were often temporary, built just for a battle. Trenches were deep, narrow pits. Troops dug them using whatever tools they could find.

Earthworks were large banks of dirt. Sometimes vines and branches were used to make them taller. Sharpened branches could be placed ahead of the earthworks. These acted like a modern **barbed-wire** fence.

THE END OF THE WAR

In April 1782, American representatives met with British officials in Paris, France. They spent the next seven months discussing an end to the American Revolution. On November 30, the two sides signed articles declaring peace.

On April 11, 1783, Congress declared an official end to the conflict with the British. In September, the British and Americans signed the Treaty of Paris. It recognized the United States of America as an independent nation.

Patriot leaders began the hard work of setting up a new government. On September 17, 1787, American leaders signed the US Constitution. It set up the framework for the new US government.

The American Revolution lasted from 1775 to 1783. Thousands of American and British troops were killed. The **technology** used during this war took many lives. But it also helped save lives. Communication technology

provided important information. And
earthworks and trenches protected
soldiers on the battlefield.

American Revolution **technology**
influenced future conflicts. Trenches
played an important role in the **American Civil War**.
The technology used in the American Revolution helped
establish a new nation. It also paved the way for future
US military successes.

It took 116 days for American leaders to outline the US Constitution before it was signed on September 17, 1787.

GLOSSARY

accurate — free from error.

allies — people, groups, or nations united for some special purpose. The major Allies in World War I were Great Britain, France, Italy, and the United States. The major Allies in World War II were Great Britain, France, the United States, and the Soviet Union.

American Civil War — the war between the Northern and Southern states from 1861 to 1865.

ammunition — bullets, shells, cartridges, or other items used in firearms and artillery.

artillery — large guns that can be used to shoot over a great distance.

barbed wire — wire that has sharp points and that is often used for fences.

cartridge — a tube containing the explosive charge and bullet or shot to be fired from a weapon.

cylinder — an object or space shaped like a tube.

dangerous — something that could hurt or harm.

debt (DEHT) — something owed to someone, especially money.

firearm — a weapon that discharges shots projected by gunpowder.

French and Indian War — the American stage of a war fought from 1754 to 1763. Great Britain fought France for control of land in North America.

friction — the force that resists motion between objects in contact.

gunpowder — a dry explosive substance that is used in firearms.

ignite — to set on fire.

petition — to make a formal request to a person of authority.

projectile — an object that can be thrown or shot out.

redoubt — a small building or area that provides soldiers with protection when under attack.

reinforcements — additional soldiers, ships, or supplies for military action.

reliable — able to be trusted to do or provide what is needed.

smoothbore — a firearm that does not have grooves in the inside of its barrel.

technology (tehk-NAH-luh-jee) — machinery and equipment developed for practical purposes using scientific principles and engineering.

trajectory — the path along which something moves through the air.

WEBSITES

To learn more about **Military Technologies**, visit **booklinks.abdopublishing.com**. These links are routinely monitored and updated to provide the most current information available.

INDEX